SWITCH YOUR MIND:
STEPS TO TAKE WHEN YOU ARE FACED WITH TRIAL AND IN TIMES OF CHALLENGES

BY

HENRY E. PARKINS

1

COPYRIGHT PAGE

TABLE OF CONTENTS

INTRODUCTION

In the journey of life, we are bound to encounter trials and challenges that test our resolve, shake our foundations, and challenge our very being. From unexpected setbacks to daunting obstacles, these moments can often feel overwhelming, leaving us feeling lost, vulnerable, and uncertain of how to navigate through the storm. Yet, it is in the crucible of adversity that our true strength and resilience are forged.

"Switch Your Mind: Steps to Take When You Are Faced with Trial and in Times of Challenges" is a guidebook crafted to illuminate the path forward when the shadows of uncertainty loom large. Within these pages, we embark on a transformative journey of self-discovery, empowerment, and growth, seeking to unravel the mysteries of the human mind and unlock the hidden reservoirs of inner strength that lie dormant within us all.

At its core, this book is a beacon of hope, a testament to the unwavering spirit that resides within each and every one of us. Through the lens of personal experience, timeless wisdom, and practical insights, we explore the intricate interplay between mindset, resilience, and the art of thriving in the face of adversity.

Drawing upon the latest research in psychology, neuroscience, and positive psychology, "Switch Your Mind" offers a roadmap for transforming the way we perceive and respond to life's challenges. We delve deep into the inner workings of the mind, unraveling the mysteries of human behavior, and uncovering the hidden patterns that shape our thoughts, emotions, and actions.

But this book is more than just a theoretical exploration of the human psyche; it is a call to action, a rallying cry for those who dare to dream, to aspire, and to defy the odds stacked against them. Through a series of practical exercises, actionable strategies, and real-life case studies, we empower readers to take control of their destiny, to rewrite the narrative of their lives, and to emerge stronger, wiser, and more resilient than ever before.

As we embark on this odyssey of self-discovery and transformation, let us remember that the journey ahead will not be easy. There will be moments of doubt, moments of fear, and moments of despair. But it is precisely in these moments that our true character is revealed, that our inner strength shines brightest, and that our capacity for growth knows no bounds.

Overview

"Switch Your Mind: Steps to Take When You Are Faced with Trial and in Times of Challenges" is a transformative guidebook designed to empower individuals to navigate through life's most daunting trials with resilience, strength, and grace. Rooted in the belief that adversity is not a roadblock but rather a pathway to growth, this book offers a comprehensive roadmap for transforming one's mindset and embracing the challenges that life presents.

At its core, "Switch Your Mind" delves into the intricate interplay between mindset and resilience, exploring how our beliefs, thoughts, and attitudes shape our experiences and responses to adversity. Through a blend of personal anecdotes, scientific insights, and practical strategies, the book illuminates the power of mindset shifts in unlocking our innate capacity for resilience and resourcefulness.

The book begins by establishing a foundational understanding of the nature of challenges, acknowledging their inevitability in the human experience and the profound impact they can have on our mental and emotional well-being. From there, readers are guided through a journey of self-discovery, introspection, and empowerment, learning to cultivate a growth-oriented mindset that thrives in the face of adversity.

"Switch Your Mind" provides readers with a wealth of practical tools and techniques for navigating through life's storms, from cultivating self-awareness and emotional regulation to fostering positive affirmations and visualization practices. Readers will discover how to embrace failure as a stepping stone to success, how to develop effective coping mechanisms for managing stress and anxiety, and how to seek support and guidance from trusted sources.

Throughout the book, readers are invited to embark on a journey of personal growth and transformation, guided by the belief that challenges are not meant to break us but to propel us towards our fullest potential. Drawing upon the latest research in psychology, neuroscience, and positive psychology, "Switch Your Mind" offers a holistic approach to resilience-building that encompasses the mind, body, and spirit.

Ultimately, "Switch Your Mind" is a testament to the indomitable human spirit and the limitless capacity for growth and renewal that resides within each of us. It is a beacon of hope for those navigating through life's darkest moments, offering practical wisdom, profound insights, and unwavering encouragement to all who dare to embark on the journey of self-discovery and transformation.

Importance of Mental Resilience in Facing Challenges

In "Switch Your Mind: Steps to Take When You Are Faced with Trial and in Times of Challenges," the significance of mental resilience in facing life's adversities cannot be overstated. Mental resilience serves as the cornerstone upon which individuals can weather storms, overcome obstacles, and emerge stronger and more empowered than before.

At its essence, mental resilience empowers individuals to adapt and thrive in the face of adversity, enabling them to bounce back from setbacks, navigate through uncertainty, and persevere in the pursuit of their goals and aspirations. In a world fraught with challenges and uncertainties, cultivating mental resilience becomes not only a valuable asset but a vital necessity for achieving personal growth and fulfillment.

One of the key benefits of mental resilience is its ability to foster a positive outlook in the midst of adversity. By cultivating resilience, individuals develop the capacity to perceive challenges not as insurmountable obstacles but as opportunities for growth and self-discovery. This shift in perspective enables individuals to approach challenges with courage, determination, and a sense of purpose, allowing them to harness their inner resources and rise above adversity.

Furthermore, mental resilience equips individuals with the emotional strength and fortitude needed to navigate through life's inevitable ups and downs. In times of crisis or uncertainty, resilient individuals are able to maintain a sense of calm and composure, effectively managing stress, anxiety, and overwhelm. By developing resilience, individuals learn to regulate their emotions, cultivate inner peace, and respond to challenges with clarity and poise.

Moreover, mental resilience fosters adaptability and flexibility in the face of change. In a rapidly evolving world, the ability to adapt to new circumstances, embrace uncertainty, and pivot in response to challenges is essential for personal and professional success. Resilient individuals possess the agility and resourcefulness needed to navigate through shifting landscapes, seize new opportunities, and chart a course towards their desired outcomes.

In addition, mental resilience strengthens interpersonal relationships and social support networks. By fostering resilience, individuals cultivate strong connections with others, build trust and mutual support, and create a sense of belonging and community. In times of adversity, resilient individuals draw upon the strength of their relationships to find solace, encouragement, and guidance, enabling them to weather even the toughest of storms.

Ultimately, mental resilience is not merely a trait to be admired but a skill to be cultivated and nurtured. In "Switch Your Mind," readers are empowered to embrace the transformative power of resilience, to cultivate a mindset of strength and resilience, and to embark on a journey of self-discovery and growth in the face of life's greatest challenges. By embracing the importance of mental resilience, readers can unlock their full potential, overcome adversity, and emerge triumphant in the pursuit of their dreams and aspirations.

In "Switch Your Mind: Steps to Take When You Are Faced with Trial and in Times of Challenges," mental resilience is defined as the capacity to adapt, bounce back, and thrive in the face of adversity, uncertainty, and setbacks. It encompasses a range of psychological attributes and coping mechanisms that enable individuals to withstand the pressures of life's challenges and emerge stronger and more empowered than before.

Mental resilience, as portrayed in the book, is not merely about enduring hardships; rather, it involves actively engaging with adversity, learning from setbacks, and harnessing inner resources to navigate through difficult circumstances. It is about cultivating a mindset of strength, courage, and resourcefulness that empowers individuals to confront obstacles head-on and persevere in the pursuit of their goals and aspirations.

At its core, mental resilience involves several key components

Positive Mindset: Mental resilience involves cultivating a positive outlook and reframing challenges as opportunities for growth and self-discovery. It entails developing the belief that setbacks are not permanent roadblocks but temporary detours on the journey towards success and fulfillment.

Emotional Regulation: Resilient individuals possess the ability to regulate their emotions effectively, maintaining a sense of calm and composure in the face of stress, anxiety, and adversity. They are able to acknowledge and process their emotions in healthy ways, without being overwhelmed or consumed by negativity.

Adaptability and Flexibility: Mental resilience entails being adaptable and flexible in response to changing circumstances. Resilient individuals are able to adjust their approach, pivot when necessary, and embrace uncertainty with courage and resilience.

Problem-Solving Skills: Resilience involves developing effective problem-solving skills and a proactive mindset towards challenges. It entails identifying solutions, seeking support when needed, and taking decisive action to overcome obstacles and achieve desired outcomes.

Social Support and Connection: Resilient individuals recognize the importance of social support and connection in times of adversity. They cultivate strong relationships, seek guidance and encouragement from others, and offer support to those in need.

17

SWITCH YOUR MIND: STEPS TO TAKE WHEN YOU ARE FACED WITH TRIAL AND IN TIMES OF CHALLENGES

CHAPTER 1

UNDERSTANDING THE NATURE OF CHALLENGES

In "Switch Your Mind: Steps to Take When You Are Faced with Trial and in Times of Challenges," delving into the nature of challenges serves as a foundational step in the journey towards resilience and personal growth. Through a deeper understanding of the complexities and nuances of challenges, individuals are better equipped to confront adversity with courage, clarity, and purpose.

At its core, understanding the nature of challenges involves acknowledging the inevitability of adversity in the human experience. Challenges come in various forms, ranging from personal setbacks and professional obstacles to societal upheavals and global crises. They test our limits, challenge our assumptions, and push us out of our comfort zones, often eliciting fear, uncertainty, and doubt.

Yet, challenges are not merely obstacles to be overcome; they are opportunities for growth, learning, and self-discovery. Within every challenge lies the potential for transformation, resilience, and empowerment. By embracing the inherent lessons and opportunities for growth embedded within challenges, individuals can harness their inner resources and emerge stronger and more resilient than before.

Moreover, understanding the nature of challenges involves recognizing the dynamic interplay between external circumstances and internal responses. While some challenges may be beyond our control, our response to those challenges is within our grasp. By cultivating a mindset of resilience, adaptability, and resourcefulness, individuals can navigate through adversity with courage, grace, and determination.

Furthermore, understanding the nature of challenges requires a willingness to embrace vulnerability and discomfort. Growth often occurs outside of our comfort zones, amidst the uncertainty and unpredictability of life's challenges. By embracing vulnerability and leaning into discomfort, individuals can cultivate the resilience needed to confront challenges head-on and emerge stronger on the other side.

In "Switch Your Mind," readers are invited to explore the multifaceted nature of challenges and to embrace them as opportunities for growth and transformation. Through introspection, self-reflection, and personal exploration, readers can deepen their understanding of the underlying dynamics of challenges and develop the resilience needed to navigate through life's storms.

Ultimately, understanding the nature of challenges is not about avoiding or minimizing adversity; rather, it is about embracing it as an integral part of the human experience. By reframing challenges as opportunities for growth and learning, individuals can cultivate the resilience needed to thrive in the face of adversity and emerge triumphant in the pursuit of their goals and aspirations.

Challenges and Trials

In "Switch Your Mind: Steps to Take When You Are Faced with Trial and in Times of Challenges," it's essential to establish a clear understanding of what constitutes challenges and trials. These terms serve as the cornerstone for recognizing and navigating through the various obstacles and adversities that life presents.

Challenges, in their broadest sense, refer to obstacles, difficulties, or hurdles that individuals encounter in their personal, professional, or spiritual journeys. These challenges can manifest in a myriad of forms, including setbacks, failures, conflicts, and uncertainties. They often disrupt the status quo, demand resilience, and test one's capacity to adapt and overcome.

Trials, on the other hand, encompass a more profound and profound level of adversity. They are often characterized by intense hardship, suffering, or tribulation, challenging individuals' beliefs, values, and sense of self. Trials may arise from external circumstances such as illness, loss, or tragedy, or they may stem from internal struggles such as doubt, fear, or inner conflict.

What distinguishes trials from ordinary challenges is their transformative power. Trials have the potential to reshape individuals' lives, catalyze profound personal growth, and deepen their understanding of themselves and the world around them. While trials may be daunting and overwhelming, they also offer opportunities for resilience, renewal, and redemption.

In "Switch Your Mind," challenges and trials serves as a foundational step in the journey towards resilience and personal growth. By gaining clarity and insight into the nature of the obstacles they face, readers can develop the resilience, courage, and wisdom needed to confront adversity head-on and emerge stronger on the other side.

Moreover, challenges and trials enables individuals to adopt a proactive mindset towards adversity. Rather than viewing challenges as insurmountable barriers or trials as tests of endurance, individuals can reframe them as opportunities for growth, learning, and self-discovery. By embracing challenges and trials as integral parts of the human experience, individuals can cultivate the resilience needed to thrive in the face of adversity and chart a course

23

towards a more fulfilling and meaningful life.

Common Types of Challenges Faced in Life

In "Switch Your Mind: Steps to Take When You Are Faced with Trial and in Times of Challenges," it is crucial to explore the common types of challenges individuals encounter in their lives. Understanding the diverse array of challenges allows readers to recognize patterns, anticipate difficulties, and develop strategies for resilience and growth.

Personal Challenges: Personal challenges encompass a wide range of obstacles related to individual well-being, relationships, and identity. These may include navigating through life transitions such as career changes, relationship issues, or personal crises. Personal challenges also encompass struggles with self-esteem, confidence, and self-identity, as well as coping with past traumas or unresolved emotional wounds.

Professional Challenges: Professional challenges arise within the context of work, career, and professional development. They may include job-related stress, workplace conflicts, job insecurity, or difficulties in achieving work-life balance. Professional challenges also encompass setbacks such as job loss, career transitions, or challenges in pursuing one's professional aspirations.

Health Challenges: Health challenges encompass physical, mental, and emotional health issues that individuals may face throughout their lives. These challenges may include chronic illnesses, acute health crises, mental health disorders, or struggles with addiction. Health challenges also encompass issues related to self-care, nutrition, fitness, and overall well-being.

Financial Challenges: Financial challenges revolve around managing finances, budgeting, and dealing with economic instability. These challenges may include debt, financial stress, unemployment, or unexpected expenses. Financial challenges also encompass issues related to financial planning, saving, and investing for the future.

Interpersonal Challenges:

Interpersonal challenges involve difficulties in relationships with family members, friends, colleagues, or romantic partners. These challenges may include communication breakdowns, conflicts, misunderstandings, or navigating through difficult conversations. Interpersonal challenges also encompass issues related to boundaries, trust, and intimacy in relationships.

Global and Societal Challenges:

Global and societal challenges encompass broader issues affecting communities, societies, and the world at large. These challenges may include social injustice, inequality, environmental degradation, political instability, or humanitarian crises. Global and societal challenges also encompass issues related to advocacy, activism, and social change.

Recognizing the Impact of Challenges on Mental Health and Well-being

In "Switch Your Mind: Steps to Take When You Are Faced with Trial and in Times of Challenges," it is imperative to recognize the profound impact that challenges can have on mental health and well-being. Acknowledging the toll that adversity takes on individuals' psychological and emotional states is the first step towards fostering resilience, healing, and growth.

Stress and Anxiety: Challenges often evoke feelings of stress and anxiety, triggering the body's natural fight-or-flight response. Persistent stress can lead to heightened levels of cortisol and adrenaline, contributing to physical symptoms such as muscle tension, headaches, and insomnia. Chronic stress and anxiety can also impair cognitive function, disrupt concentration, and interfere with daily functioning.

Depression and Hopelessness: Prolonged exposure to challenges can also contribute to feelings of depression,

27

hopelessness, and despair. Individuals may experience a sense of powerlessness, loss of motivation, and diminished interest in activities they once enjoyed. Depression can manifest in physical symptoms such as fatigue, changes in appetite, and persistent feelings of sadness or emptiness.

Self-esteem and Self-worth: Challenges can profoundly impact individuals' sense of self-esteem and self-worth. Setbacks and failures may trigger feelings of inadequacy, self-doubt, and shame. Individuals may question their abilities, worthiness, and value as human beings. Low self-esteem can undermine confidence, resilience, and the ability to persevere in the face of adversity.

Relationship Strain: Challenges can strain interpersonal relationships, leading to conflicts, misunderstandings, and breakdowns in communication. Stress, anxiety, and emotional distress may spill over into relationships, causing tension and friction with family members, friends, or colleagues. Difficulty in navigating through challenges together can erode trust, intimacy, and connection in relationships.

Isolation and Loneliness: Facing challenges can also contribute to feelings of isolation and loneliness. Individuals may withdraw from social interactions, feeling misunderstood, unsupported, or disconnected from others. Isolation can exacerbate feelings of despair and hopelessness, further compounding the impact of challenges on mental health and well-being.

In "Switch Your Mind," recognizing the impact of challenges on mental health and well-being serves as a call to action for readers to prioritize self-care, seek support, and cultivate resilience in the face of adversity. By acknowledging the emotional toll of challenges, readers can validate their experiences, normalize their feelings, and take proactive steps towards healing and growth.

Moreover, recognizing the impact of challenges on mental health and well-being underscores the importance of destigmatizing mental health issues and promoting open dialogue surrounding mental health struggles. By fostering empathy, compassion, and understanding, individuals can create supportive communities where individuals feel safe to seek help, share their experiences, and embark on the journey towards healing and recovery.

Ultimately, by recognizing the impact of challenges on mental health and well-being, readers of "Switch Your Mind" can begin to cultivate the resilience, self-compassion, and inner strength needed to navigate through life's storms and emerge stronger and more empowered on the other side.

CHAPTER 2

THE POWER OF MINDSET SHIFT

In "Switch Your Mind: Steps to Take When You Are Faced with Trial and in Times of Challenges," the concept of mindset shift emerges as a pivotal tool for navigating through adversity with resilience, courage, and clarity. Mindset, the lens through which individuals perceive and interpret the world, plays a central role in shaping their responses to challenges and setbacks.

Fixed vs. Growth Mindset: At the heart of mindset shift lies the distinction between a fixed mindset and a growth mindset. Individuals with a fixed mindset believe that their abilities, intelligence, and talents are fixed traits that cannot be changed. In contrast, individuals with a growth mindset believe that their abilities can be developed through dedication, effort, and perseverance. By embracing a growth mindset, individuals open themselves up to new possibilities, challenges, and opportunities for growth.

Reframing Challenges as Opportunities: Mindset shift involves reframing challenges as opportunities for learning, growth, and self-discovery. Rather than viewing challenges as insurmountable obstacles, individuals with a growth mindset approach them as valuable learning experiences that can foster resilience, creativity, and innovation. By reframing challenges in this way, individuals empower themselves to embrace adversity with courage and determination.

Embracing the Power of Positive Thinking: Mindset shift also entails embracing the power of positive thinking and optimism in the face of adversity. Positive thinking involves cultivating a mindset of hope, resilience, and gratitude, even in the midst of difficult circumstances. By focusing on what is within their control and maintaining a positive outlook, individuals can harness the transformative power of optimism to navigate through challenges with grace and resilience.

Cultivating Self-Compassion and Self-Kindness:

Mindset shift involves cultivating self-compassion and self-kindness towards oneself in times of adversity. Rather than engaging in self-criticism or blame, individuals with a growth mindset practice self-compassion by treating themselves with kindness, understanding, and acceptance. By acknowledging their inherent worth and value as human beings, individuals can develop the resilience needed to weather life's storms with grace and dignity.

Challenging Limiting Beliefs and Assumptions:

Mindset shift requires individuals to challenge limiting beliefs and assumptions that may be holding them back from realizing their full potential. By questioning negative self-talk, self-limiting beliefs, and assumptions about their capabilities, individuals can break free from the constraints of their own minds and embrace a more expansive and empowering worldview.

The Concept of Mindset

In "Switch Your Mind: Steps to Take When You Are Faced with Trial and in Times of Challenges," the concept of mindset serves as a cornerstone for understanding how individuals perceive, interpret, and respond to the challenges they encounter in life. Mindset, as explored in the book, encompasses the underlying beliefs, attitudes, and assumptions that shape individuals' thoughts, behaviors, and emotional responses.

Fixed vs. Growth Mindset: Central to the concept of mindset is the distinction between a fixed mindset and a growth mindset. Individuals with a fixed mindset believe that their abilities, intelligence, and talents are innate traits that cannot be changed. They may view challenges as threats to their sense of self-worth and competence, leading them to avoid risks and shy away from opportunities for growth. In contrast, individuals with a growth mindset believe that their abilities can be developed through effort, perseverance, and learning. They embrace challenges as opportunities for growth, viewing setbacks as temporary setbacks rather than permanent reflections of their capabilities.

The Power of Belief: Mindset shapes individuals' beliefs about their own potential and the world around them. Believing in one's ability to learn, grow, and overcome obstacles is a hallmark of a growth mindset. By cultivating a belief in the power of effort and resilience, individuals can unleash their full potential and achieve greater success and fulfillment in life.

The Influence of Mindset on Behavior: Mindset influences individuals' behaviors and actions in response to challenges. Those with a growth mindset are more likely to approach challenges with curiosity, persistence, and determination. They embrace failure as a natural part of the learning process and are willing to take risks in pursuit of their goals. In contrast, individuals with a fixed mindset may avoid challenges or give up easily in the face of adversity, fearing failure and rejection.

The Role of Mindset in Resilience: Mindset plays a critical role in determining individuals' resilience in the face of adversity. Those with a growth mindset are better equipped to bounce back from setbacks, setbacks, and setbacks. They view challenges as opportunities for learning and personal growth, enabling them to navigate through life's storms with courage, resilience, and grace.

Cultivating a Growth Mindset: In "Switch Your Mind," readers are encouraged to cultivate a growth mindset as a pathway to personal transformation and resilience. By embracing the belief that their abilities can be developed through dedication, effort, and perseverance, readers can unlock their full potential and overcome even the most daunting challenges. Through self-reflection, positive affirmations, and intentional practice, individuals can shift their mindset towards one of growth, possibility, and empowerment.

In essence, the concept of mindset in "Switch Your Mind" underscores the transformative power of belief, resilience, and self-discovery. By embracing a growth mindset, readers can transcend limitations, overcome obstacles, and chart a course towards a life filled with purpose, resilience, and fulfillment. Mindset serves as a guiding principle for navigating through life's trials and challenges with courage, clarity, and grace.

The Role of Mindset in Overcoming Challenges

In "Switch Your Mind: Steps to Take When You Are Faced with Trial and in Times of Challenges," delving into the role of mindset serves as a pivotal exploration in understanding how individuals navigate and triumph over adversities. The mindset individuals adopt profoundly influences their perceptions, attitudes, and responses to challenges they encounter throughout life.

Perception of Challenges: Mindset shapes how individuals perceive challenges. Those with a growth mindset view challenges as opportunities for growth, learning, and self-improvement. They see obstacles as temporary roadblocks that can be overcome with effort and perseverance. Conversely, individuals with a fixed mindset may perceive challenges as threats to their abilities and self-worth, leading to avoidance and a fear of failure.

Resilience and Persistence: Mindset plays a crucial role in determining individuals' resilience and persistence in the face of challenges. Those with a growth mindset are more resilient and persistent, as they believe in their capacity to learn and improve over time. They approach challenges with a sense of optimism and determination, viewing setbacks as valuable learning experiences. In contrast, individuals with a fixed mindset may be more prone to giving up easily when faced with obstacles, as they perceive failure as a reflection of their inherent limitations.

Embracing Failure as a Learning Opportunity: Mindset influences how individuals interpret and respond to failure. Those with a growth mindset embrace failure as a natural part of the learning process. They view setbacks as opportunities to gain valuable insights, refine their strategies, and ultimately grow stronger. By reframing failure as a stepping stone to success, individuals with a growth mindset remain resilient and motivated in the face of adversity.

Adopting a Solution-Oriented Approach: Mindset guides individuals in adopting a solution-oriented approach to challenges. Those with a growth mindset focus on finding solutions and taking proactive steps towards overcoming obstacles. They seek out support, explore alternative strategies, and remain open to feedback and constructive criticism. By maintaining a solution-oriented mindset, individuals can navigate through challenges with creativity, resourcefulness, and determination.

Cultivating Self-Compassion and Self-Kindness: Mindset influences how individuals treat themselves during times of adversity. Those with a growth mindset practice self-compassion and self-kindness, recognizing that setbacks and challenges are a natural part of the human experience. They respond to setbacks with patience, understanding, and self-encouragement, rather than harsh self-criticism or judgment. By cultivating self-compassion, individuals can nurture their resilience and inner strength, enabling them to persevere through life's trials with grace and dignity.

CHAPTER 3

PRACTICAL STRATEGIES FOR MINDSET TRANSFORMATION

In "Switch Your Mind: Steps to Take When You Are Faced with Trial and in Times of Challenges," practical strategies for mindset transformation are essential tools for empowering individuals to navigate through adversity with resilience, courage, and clarity. These strategies offer actionable steps for cultivating a growth-oriented mindset and embracing challenges as opportunities for growth and self-discovery.

Mindfulness and Self-Awareness: Cultivating mindfulness and self-awareness is a foundational step in mindset transformation. Mindfulness practices such as meditation, deep breathing exercises, and body scans can help individuals cultivate present-moment awareness and observe their thoughts, emotions, and beliefs without judgment. By developing self-awareness, individuals can identify limiting beliefs and thought patterns that may be holding them back from adopting a growth mindset.

Positive Affirmations and Visualization: Positive affirmations and visualization techniques are powerful tools for rewiring the subconscious mind and cultivating a positive mindset. Encouraging individuals to create affirmations that reflect their goals, strengths, and values can help reinforce positive beliefs and attitudes. Visualization exercises, where individuals imagine themselves overcoming challenges and achieving their desired outcomes, can further enhance their sense of self-efficacy and resilience.

Embracing Failure as a Learning Opportunity: Encouraging individuals to reframe failure as a natural and necessary part of the learning process is essential for mindset transformation. Rather than viewing failure as a reflection of their abilities or self-worth, individuals can embrace it as a valuable learning opportunity. Encouraging individuals to reflect on past failures, extract lessons learned, and identify areas for growth can help cultivate resilience and perseverance in the face of adversity.

Setting Realistic Goals and Action Plans: Setting realistic goals and action plans is crucial for maintaining motivation and momentum in the pursuit of personal growth. Encouraging individuals to set specific, measurable, achievable, relevant, and time-bound (SMART) goals can help clarify their intentions and focus their efforts. Breaking goals down into smaller, actionable steps can make them more manageable and achievable, increasing individuals' confidence and sense of progress along their journey.

Seeking Support and Accountability: Encouraging individuals to seek support and accountability from trusted friends, family members, or mentors can provide valuable encouragement and guidance on their journey towards mindset transformation. Accountability partners can help individuals stay accountable to their goals, celebrate their successes, and navigate through challenges with resilience and determination.

43

Practicing Gratitude and Self-Compassion: Practicing gratitude and self-compassion is essential for nurturing a positive mindset and resilience in the face of adversity. Encouraging individuals to cultivate a daily gratitude practice, where they reflect on the blessings and positive aspects of their lives, can help shift their focus from scarcity to abundance. Similarly, fostering self-compassion and kindness towards oneself in times of difficulty can help individuals navigate through challenges with grace and resilience.

In "Switch Your Mind," readers are empowered to explore and implement practical strategies for mindset transformation as a pathway to personal growth and resilience. By embracing these strategies, individuals can cultivate a growth-oriented mindset, navigate through challenges with courage and determination, and emerge stronger and more empowered than before. Mindset transformation serves as a guiding principle for unlocking individuals' full potential and embracing the transformative power of resilience and self-discovery.

Cultivating Self-Awareness and Emotional Regulation

In "Switch Your Mind: Steps to Take When You Are Faced with Trial and in Times of Challenges," the cultivation of self-awareness and emotional regulation emerges as fundamental practices for navigating through adversity with resilience, clarity, and grace. These practices empower individuals to develop a deeper understanding of their thoughts, emotions, and behaviors, and to respond to challenges with intentionality and self-compassion.

Self-Reflection and Mindfulness: Cultivating self-awareness begins with self-reflection and mindfulness practices. Encouraging individuals to set aside time for introspection, journaling, or meditation can help them tune into their inner experiences and gain insight into their thoughts, emotions, and beliefs. Mindfulness practices promote present-moment awareness and non-judgmental acceptance of one's internal experiences,

45

fostering greater self-awareness and emotional clarity.

Identifying Triggers and Patterns:

Developing self-awareness involves identifying triggers and patterns that influence one's thoughts, emotions, and behaviors. Encouraging individuals to reflect on past experiences and identify recurring themes, triggers, and emotional patterns can help them gain insight into their reactions to challenges. By recognizing these patterns, individuals can develop strategies for managing their responses and cultivating greater emotional resilience.

Emotional Regulation Techniques:

Emotional regulation techniques empower individuals to manage and navigate through difficult emotions effectively. Encouraging individuals to practice deep breathing exercises, progressive muscle relaxation, or visualization techniques can help regulate the body's stress response and promote emotional balance. Additionally, encouraging individuals to engage in activities that promote relaxation and stress reduction, such as spending time in nature, practicing hobbies, or engaging in physical activity, can help regulate emotions and promote overall well-being.

Cognitive Restructuring:

Cognitive restructuring involves challenging and reframing negative or distorted thinking patterns that contribute to emotional distress. Encouraging individuals to examine their thoughts and beliefs about themselves, others, and the world can help them identify and challenge cognitive distortions, such as all-or-nothing thinking, catastrophizing, or personalization. By replacing negative thoughts with more balanced and realistic interpretations, individuals can cultivate a more adaptive and resilient mindset in the face of challenges.

Developing Self-Compassion and Acceptance:

Cultivating self-awareness involves developing self-compassion and acceptance towards oneself in times of difficulty. Encouraging individuals to practice self-compassion exercises, such as writing self-affirmations or practicing self-care activities, can help cultivate a kind and nurturing inner dialogue. Additionally, encouraging individuals to practice acceptance and non-judgment

47

towards their thoughts, emotions, and experiences can help foster greater emotional resilience and self-acceptance.

Adopting Positive Affirmations and Visualization Techniques

In "Switch Your Mind: Steps to Take When You Are Faced with Trial and in Times of Challenges," adopting positive affirmations and visualization techniques emerges as powerful practices for cultivating a resilient mindset and navigating through adversity with courage, clarity, and optimism. These techniques empower individuals to harness the power of their thoughts and beliefs to create positive change and transformation in their lives.

Positive Affirmations: Positive affirmations are empowering statements that affirm one's strengths, values, and aspirations. Encouraging individuals to adopt positive affirmations involves identifying and affirming their inherent worth, resilience, and capacity for growth. Affirmations such as "I am resilient," "I am capable of overcoming challenges," and "I embrace opportunities for growth" can help individuals cultivate a positive mindset and foster self-confidence in the face of adversity. By repeating affirmations regularly, individuals reinforce positive beliefs and attitudes, ultimately shaping their perceptions and responses to challenges.

Visualization Techniques: Visualization techniques involve mentally rehearsing desired outcomes and experiences in vivid detail. Encouraging individuals to engage in visualization exercises involves guiding them to imagine themselves successfully overcoming challenges and achieving their goals. Visualization techniques can help individuals clarify their intentions, boost their motivation, and cultivate a sense of empowerment and self-efficacy. By visualizing themselves navigating through challenges with grace and resilience, individuals prime their minds for success and foster a sense of confidence and optimism in their abilities.

Creating Vision Boards: Vision boards are visual representations of individuals' goals, dreams, and aspirations. Encouraging individuals to create vision boards involves gathering images, quotes, and symbols that inspire and motivate them towards their desired outcomes. Vision boards serve as powerful visual reminders of individuals' aspirations and can help reinforce positive beliefs and intentions. By regularly reviewing their vision boards, individuals keep their goals at the forefront of their minds and stay aligned with their aspirations, even in the face of challenges and setbacks.

Practicing Gratitude Affirmations: Gratitude affirmations involve expressing appreciation for the blessings and positive aspects of one's life. Encouraging individuals to practice gratitude affirmations involves acknowledging and affirming the abundance and richness of their experiences, relationships, and accomplishments. Gratitude affirmations such as "I am grateful for the love and support in my life" and "I appreciate the lessons and growth opportunities in challenges" help individuals cultivate a positive mindset and foster resilience in the face of adversity. By focusing on what is going well in their lives, individuals shift their perspective from scarcity to abundance and cultivate a sense of optimism and gratitude.

Embracing a Solution-Oriented Mindset

In "Switch Your Mind: Steps to Take When You Are Faced with Trial and in Times of Challenges," embracing a solution-oriented mindset emerges as a key principle for navigating through adversity with resilience, clarity, and effectiveness. This mindset empowers individuals to approach challenges as opportunities for growth and problem-solving, enabling them to overcome obstacles and thrive in the face of adversity.

Focus on Solutions: Embracing a solution-oriented mindset involves shifting focus from problems to solutions. Rather than dwelling on the challenges and obstacles they face, individuals focus their energy and attention on identifying actionable steps and strategies for addressing them. By adopting a proactive and problem-solving approach, individuals empower themselves to take control of their circumstances and work towards positive outcomes.

Seeking Opportunities for Growth: Embracing a solution-oriented mindset entails viewing challenges as opportunities for growth and learning. Rather than seeing setbacks as roadblocks, individuals see them as valuable lessons and experiences that contribute to their personal and professional development. By reframing challenges in this way, individuals cultivate resilience, adaptability, and a willingness to embrace change and uncertainty.

Creative Problem-Solving: Embracing a solution-oriented mindset involves engaging in creative problem-solving techniques to overcome obstacles and achieve desired outcomes. Individuals are encouraged to think outside the box, explore alternative approaches, and collaborate with others to find innovative solutions to complex problems. By harnessing their creativity and resourcefulness, individuals can overcome even the most daunting challenges and achieve meaningful progress towards their goals.

Taking Action: Embracing a solution-oriented mindset is not just about thinking positively; it's about taking decisive action to implement solutions and effect positive change. Individuals are encouraged to break down their goals into manageable tasks, prioritize action steps, and take consistent and deliberate action towards their objectives. By taking proactive steps towards solutions, individuals gain momentum, build confidence, and make meaningful progress towards overcoming challenges.

Learning from Feedback and Reflection: Embracing a solution-oriented mindset involves being open to feedback and reflection as essential components of the problem-solving process. Individuals seek out feedback from others, learn from their experiences, and adapt their strategies based on lessons learned. By embracing a growth mindset and viewing feedback as an opportunity for improvement, individuals continuously evolve and refine their approaches to problem-solving.

Building Resilience through Acceptance and Adaptation

In "Switch Your Mind: Steps to Take When You Are Faced with Trial and in Times of Challenges," building resilience through acceptance and adaptation emerges as a transformative practice for navigating through adversity with grace, courage, and inner strength. This approach empowers individuals to embrace change, cultivate flexibility, and find meaning and growth in the face of life's inevitable challenges.

Acceptance of Reality: Building resilience begins with acceptance of reality as it is, rather than as we wish it to be. Acceptance involves acknowledging and coming to terms with the challenges, setbacks, and uncertainties that life presents. Rather than resisting or denying reality, individuals embrace the present moment with openness, curiosity, and compassion. By accepting reality as it unfolds, individuals free themselves from the burden of resistance and open themselves up to new possibilities and opportunities for growth.

54

Cultivating Emotional Resilience: Building resilience through acceptance involves cultivating emotional resilience in the face of adversity. This entails acknowledging and validating one's emotions, even in the midst of difficult circumstances. Rather than suppressing or avoiding painful emotions, individuals allow themselves to feel and express their emotions in healthy and constructive ways. By honoring their emotional experiences with kindness and self-compassion, individuals strengthen their resilience and capacity to cope with life's challenges.

Flexibility and Adaptation: Building resilience through adaptation involves cultivating flexibility and adaptability in response to changing circumstances. Rather than clinging rigidly to preconceived expectations or plans, individuals remain open to new information, perspectives, and possibilities. They embrace uncertainty as an inherent part of the human experience and adapt their strategies and approaches accordingly. By cultivating flexibility and adaptability, individuals navigate through challenges with agility, creativity, and resilience.

Finding Meaning and Purpose: Building resilience through acceptance and adaptation involves finding meaning and purpose in the midst of adversity. Rather than viewing challenges as random or meaningless events, individuals seek out opportunities for growth, learning, and self-discovery. They cultivate a sense of purpose that transcends immediate difficulties and aligns with their values, passions, and aspirations. By infusing their experiences with meaning and purpose, individuals derive strength and resilience from even the most challenging circumstances.

Seeking Support and Connection: Building resilience through acceptance and adaptation involves seeking support and connection from others during times of adversity. Rather than facing challenges alone, individuals reach out to friends, family members, mentors, or support groups for guidance, encouragement, and perspective. They draw strength from their relationships and connections, knowing that they are not alone in their struggles.

By fostering supportive relationships and community, individuals build resilience through shared experiences and collective wisdom.

CHAPTER 4

DEVELOPING EFFECTIVE COPING MECHANISMS

In "Switch Your Mind: Steps to Take When You Are Faced with Trial and in Times of Challenges," the development of effective coping mechanisms emerges as a crucial aspect of navigating through adversity with resilience, clarity, and grace. Coping mechanisms empower individuals to manage stress, regulate emotions, and adapt to challenging circumstances, ultimately fostering inner strength and well-being.

Identifying Individual Stressors: Developing effective coping mechanisms begins with identifying individual stressors and triggers that contribute to feelings of distress and overwhelm. Encouraging individuals to reflect on their experiences and recognize patterns of stress and anxiety can help them gain insight into their unique stressors. By identifying specific stressors, individuals can develop targeted coping strategies to manage their responses and alleviate distress.

Exploring Healthy Coping Strategies: Developing effective coping mechanisms involves exploring healthy coping strategies that promote resilience and well-being. Encouraging individuals to engage in activities that promote relaxation, stress reduction, and emotional regulation, such as mindfulness meditation, deep breathing exercises, or physical exercise, can help them manage stress and promote emotional balance. Additionally, encouraging individuals to engage in hobbies, creative outlets, or social activities that bring them joy and fulfillment can serve as powerful coping mechanisms during difficult times.

Building a Support Network: Developing effective coping mechanisms involves building a support network of friends, family members, mentors, or support groups who can provide emotional support, guidance, and encouragement during times of adversity. Encouraging individuals to reach out to trusted individuals for support, share their experiences, and seek guidance can help them feel understood, validated, and supported in their journey. By fostering

59

connections and community, individuals can draw strength from their relationships and navigate through challenges with resilience and grace.

Practicing Self-Compassion and Self-Care:
Developing effective coping mechanisms involves practicing self-compassion and self-care as essential components of well-being. Encouraging individuals to prioritize self-care activities, such as adequate sleep, healthy nutrition, and regular exercise, can help promote physical and emotional resilience. Additionally, encouraging individuals to practice self-compassion by treating themselves with kindness, understanding, and acceptance during times of difficulty can help alleviate feelings of guilt, shame, or self-criticism.

Seeking Professional Support:
Developing effective coping mechanisms may also involve seeking professional support from mental health professionals, counselors, or therapists when needed. Encouraging individuals to seek professional support can provide them with tools, resources, and strategies for managing stress, navigating challenges,

and promoting mental health and well-being. By seeking professional support, individuals can gain insight into their experiences, learn coping skills, and receive guidance on their journey towards healing and growth.

Identifying Healthy Coping Mechanisms

In "Switch Your Mind: Steps to Take When You Are Faced with Trial and in Times of Challenges," the identification of healthy coping mechanisms is paramount to navigating adversity with resilience, clarity, and inner strength. Healthy coping mechanisms empower individuals to effectively manage stress, regulate emotions, and foster overall well-being in the face of life's challenges. Here are key aspects of identifying and implementing healthy coping mechanisms:

Self-Awareness and Reflection: The process of identifying healthy coping mechanisms begins with self-awareness and reflection. Individuals are encouraged to reflect on their experiences, emotions, and reactions to stressors. By tuning into their thoughts and feelings, individuals can gain insight into their coping strategies and identify patterns of behavior that may be helpful or harmful.

Understanding Personal Needs: Identifying healthy coping mechanisms involves understanding personal needs and preferences. What works for one individual may not work for another. Encouraging individuals to explore a variety of coping strategies, such as mindfulness practices, physical exercise, creative expression, or spending time in nature, allows them to discover what resonates most with their unique needs and preferences.

Promoting Emotional Regulation: Healthy coping mechanisms promote emotional regulation and resilience in the face of adversity. Strategies such as deep breathing exercises, progressive muscle relaxation, or journaling can help individuals manage intense emotions and reduce stress levels. By cultivating emotional awareness and regulation skills, individuals can respond to challenges with greater calmness and clarity.

Encouraging Positive Lifestyle Choices: Healthy coping mechanisms encompass positive lifestyle choices that support overall well-being. Encouraging individuals to prioritize adequate sleep, nutritious eating, regular physical activity, and healthy relationships fosters resilience and vitality. Engaging in activities that promote relaxation and pleasure, such as hobbies, leisure activities, and spending time with loved ones, contributes to emotional balance and fulfillment.

Seeking Professional Guidance: Identifying healthy coping mechanisms may also involve seeking professional guidance and support when needed. Mental health professionals, counselors, or therapists can offer insight, guidance, and tools for managing stress, navigating challenges, and promoting mental well-being. Encouraging individuals to reach out for professional support demonstrates strength and self-awareness in prioritizing their mental and emotional health.

Cultivating a Supportive Environment: Creating a supportive environment that fosters healthy coping mechanisms is essential. Encouraging open communication, empathy, and validation within personal and professional relationships cultivates a sense of safety and belonging. Building a supportive network of friends, family members, or support groups provides opportunities for connection, validation, and mutual support during times of difficulty.

Strategies for Managing Stress and Anxiety

In "Switch Your Mind: Steps to Take When You Are Faced with Trial and in Times of Challenges," implementing effective strategies for managing stress and anxiety is pivotal to navigating adversity with resilience, clarity, and inner peace. These strategies empower individuals to cultivate emotional balance, promote well-being, and thrive amidst life's challenges. Here are key approaches to managing stress and anxiety:

Mindfulness Meditation: Mindfulness meditation is a powerful practice for managing stress and anxiety by fostering present-moment awareness and inner calmness. Encouraging individuals to engage in mindfulness meditation, even for a few minutes each day, allows them to observe their thoughts and emotions without judgment, thereby reducing the impact of stressors on their well-being.

Deep Breathing Exercises:

Deep breathing exercises are simple yet effective techniques for reducing stress and anxiety by activating the body's relaxation response. Encouraging individuals to practice deep breathing exercises, such as diaphragmatic breathing or square breathing, helps regulate the nervous system and promote feelings of calmness and relaxation during times of distress.

Physical Activity:

Regular physical activity is a natural antidote to stress and anxiety, as it releases endorphins and reduces the body's stress hormones. Encouraging individuals to engage in physical activities they enjoy, such as walking, jogging, yoga, or dancing, provides a healthy outlet for pent-up energy and tension, promoting emotional well-being and resilience.

Cognitive Behavioral Techniques:

Cognitive behavioral techniques involve identifying and challenging negative thought patterns that contribute to stress and anxiety. Encouraging individuals to practice cognitive restructuring, where they challenge irrational beliefs and replace them with more balanced and realistic thoughts, helps alleviate anxiety and promote a sense of control over one's circumstances.

Setting Boundaries and Priorities: Setting boundaries and priorities is essential for managing stress and preventing burnout. Encouraging individuals to prioritize tasks, delegate responsibilities, and say no to excessive demands on their time and energy helps preserve their mental and emotional well-being. By establishing healthy boundaries, individuals create space for self-care and meaningful activities that nourish their resilience and vitality.

Seeking Social Support: Social support is a powerful buffer against stress and anxiety, as it provides a sense of connection, belonging, and validation. Encouraging individuals to reach out to friends, family members, or support groups for emotional support and guidance fosters resilience and strengthens interpersonal relationships. By sharing their experiences and receiving empathy and understanding from others, individuals feel less isolated and better equipped to cope with life's challenges.

Practicing Self-Care: Practicing self-care is essential for managing stress and anxiety and promoting overall well-being. Encouraging individuals to prioritize self-care activities, such as adequate sleep, nutritious eating, relaxation techniques, and engaging in hobbies or leisure activities, helps replenish their physical, emotional, and mental resources. By nurturing themselves with kindness and compassion, individuals build resilience and capacity to navigate through adversity with grace and strength.

Seeking Support from Friends, Family, and Professionals

In "Switch Your Mind: Steps to Take When You Are Faced with Trial and in Times of Challenges," the importance of seeking support from friends, family, and professionals emerges as a cornerstone for navigating through adversity with resilience, clarity, and strength. This support network provides individuals with valuable resources, guidance, and empathy, empowering them to overcome obstacles and thrive amidst life's challenges. Here are key aspects of seeking support:

Emotional Validation and Understanding: Seeking support from friends, family, and loved ones provides individuals with emotional validation and understanding during times of difficulty. Sharing their experiences, thoughts, and feelings with trusted confidants allows individuals to feel heard, validated, and supported in their journey. Knowing that they are not alone in their struggles helps individuals navigate through adversity with greater resilience and courage.

Practical Guidance and Advice: Friends, family members, and mentors can offer practical guidance and advice based on their own experiences and perspectives. Encouraging individuals to seek advice and perspective from trusted sources helps broaden their understanding of their challenges and explore potential solutions and strategies for coping. Whether it's seeking career advice, relationship guidance, or emotional support, having a supportive network of individuals to turn to provides individuals with valuable insights and encouragement.

Professional Expertise and Guidance:

In addition to seeking support from friends and family, individuals may benefit from seeking guidance from mental health professionals, counselors, or therapists. These professionals offer specialized expertise and tools for managing stress, coping with emotions, and navigating through challenging circumstances. Encouraging individuals to seek professional support demonstrates strength and self-awareness in prioritizing their mental and emotional well-being.

Creating a Safe and Non-Judgmental Space:

Seeking support from friends, family, and professionals involves creating a safe and non-judgmental space for open communication and vulnerability. Encouraging individuals to express themselves authentically and honestly fosters deeper connections and mutual understanding. Creating a supportive environment where individuals feel

69

accepted, respected, and valued enables them to share their struggles and seek guidance without fear of judgment or criticism.

Building Resilience Through Connection: Seeking support from friends, family, and professionals strengthens interpersonal relationships and builds resilience through connection. Engaging in meaningful conversations, offering empathy and support, and receiving encouragement and validation from others fosters a sense of belonging and connectedness. Knowing that they have a support network to lean on during challenging times bolsters individuals' resilience and empowers them to face adversity with courage and determination.

In "Switch Your Mind," readers are encouraged to seek support from friends, family, and professionals as an essential aspect of navigating through life's challenges with resilience and empowerment. By cultivating supportive relationships, seeking guidance from trusted sources, and creating a safe and non-judgmental space for open communication, individuals build resilience and strength in the face of adversity. Seeking support enables individuals to embrace the journey towards personal growth and transformation with courage, grace, and resilience.

Practicing Self-Care and Mindfulness Techniques

In "Switch Your Mind: Steps to Take When You Are Faced with Trial and in Times of Challenges," the integration of self-care and mindfulness techniques stands as a foundational practice for navigating adversity with resilience, clarity, and inner peace. These practices empower individuals to nurture their well-being, cultivate emotional balance, and develop a deeper connection with themselves amidst life's challenges. Here's an exploration of practicing self-care and mindfulness techniques:

Self-Compassion and Acceptance: Practicing self-care begins with self-compassion and acceptance. Encouraging individuals to treat themselves with kindness, understanding, and acceptance during difficult times fosters resilience and emotional well-being. By acknowledging their struggles with self-compassion, individuals create space for healing and growth, cultivating a sense of inner strength and self-worth.

Prioritizing Physical Well-Being: Self-care involves prioritizing physical well-being through nourishing practices such as adequate sleep, nutritious eating, and regular exercise. Encouraging individuals to prioritize sleep hygiene, mindful eating, and physical activity promotes vitality and resilience, providing a strong foundation for navigating through challenges with energy and vitality.

Mindfulness Meditation: Mindfulness meditation is a powerful practice for cultivating present-moment awareness and inner calmness. Encouraging individuals to engage in mindfulness meditation, even for a few minutes each day, allows them to observe their thoughts and emotions with curiosity and non-judgment, reducing the impact of stressors on their well-being. By anchoring themselves in the present moment, individuals cultivate resilience and clarity amidst life's uncertainties.

Breath Awareness and Relaxation Techniques: Breath awareness and relaxation techniques offer simple yet effective strategies for managing stress and promoting relaxation. Encouraging individuals to practice deep breathing exercises, progressive muscle relaxation, or guided imagery techniques helps regulate the body's stress response and promote emotional balance. By connecting with their breath and relaxing their body, individuals create a sense of calmness and ease amidst life's challenges.

Engaging in Meaningful Activities: Self-care involves engaging in activities that bring joy, fulfillment, and meaning into one's life. Encouraging individuals to pursue hobbies, creative outlets, or leisure activities that nourish their soul and uplift their spirits promotes emotional well-being and resilience. Whether it's spending time in nature, pursuing artistic endeavors, or connecting with loved ones, engaging in meaningful activities enhances individuals' sense of purpose and vitality.

Setting Boundaries and Saying No: Practicing self-care involves setting boundaries and saying no to excessive demands on one's time and energy. Encouraging individuals to prioritize their needs, delegate tasks, and assert their boundaries promotes balance and prevents burnout. By honoring their limits and respecting their needs, individuals preserve their well-being and cultivate resilience amidst life's demands.

CHAPTER 5

NAVIGATING THROUGH ADVERSITY

In "Switch Your Mind: Steps to Take When You Are Faced with Trial and in Times of Challenges," the journey of navigating through adversity is illuminated as a transformative process of growth, resilience, and self-discovery. This journey empowers individuals to confront challenges with courage, clarity, and grace, ultimately emerging stronger, wiser, and more empowered than before. Here's an exploration of navigating through adversity:

Acknowledging the Reality of Adversity: Navigating through adversity begins with acknowledging the reality of challenges and setbacks. Encouraging individuals to confront their struggles with honesty and courage allows them to face adversity head-on, rather than denying or avoiding difficult truths. By acknowledging the presence of adversity, individuals take the first step towards resilience and growth.

75

Cultivating Resilience and Adaptability: Navigating through adversity involves cultivating resilience and adaptability in response to changing circumstances. Encouraging individuals to embrace change, learn from setbacks, and adapt their strategies empowers them to overcome obstacles and thrive amidst adversity. By cultivating resilience, individuals develop the inner strength and flexibility needed to navigate life's challenges with courage and determination.

Seeking Support and Connection: Navigating through adversity involves seeking support and connection from friends, family, and professionals. Encouraging individuals to reach out for support, share their experiences, and seek guidance fosters resilience and strengthens interpersonal relationships. By building a support network, individuals find solace, validation, and encouragement amidst life's storms, empowering them to face adversity with greater confidence and resilience.

Finding Meaning and Purpose: Navigating through adversity invites individuals to find meaning and purpose in their experiences. Encouraging individuals to search for lessons, growth opportunities, and silver linings in adversity helps them derive meaning from challenging circumstances. By infusing their experiences with purpose and significance, individuals transform adversity into a catalyst for personal growth, wisdom, and self-discovery.

Embracing Self-Compassion and Acceptance: Navigating through adversity involves embracing self-compassion and acceptance towards oneself. Encouraging individuals to treat themselves with kindness, understanding, and acceptance during difficult times fosters resilience and emotional well-being. By practicing self-compassion, individuals cultivate inner strength, self-worth, and resilience amidst adversity.

Embracing the Journey of Growth and Transformation: Navigating through adversity is ultimately a journey of growth and transformation. Encouraging individuals to embrace the journey with openness, curiosity, and courage allows them to discover their inner resilience, wisdom, and potential. By viewing adversity as a pathway to growth and self-discovery, individuals emerge from challenges stronger, wiser, and more empowered than before.

In "Switch Your Mind," readers are empowered to navigate through adversity as a transformative journey of resilience, courage, and self-discovery. By acknowledging the reality of challenges, cultivating resilience, seeking support and connection, finding meaning and purpose, embracing self-compassion, and embracing the journey of growth and transformation, individuals navigate through adversity with grace, courage, and resilience. Navigating through adversity enables individuals to embrace the journey towards personal growth and empowerment, ultimately emerging stronger, wiser, and more resilient than before.

Embracing Failure as a Learning Opportunity

In "Switch Your Mind: Steps to Take When You Are Faced with Trial and in Times of

Challenges," the concept of embracing failure as a learning opportunity emerges as a transformative mindset shift for navigating through adversity with resilience, clarity, and growth. Instead of viewing failure as a setback or a sign of inadequacy, individuals are encouraged to reframe failure as an essential stepping stone on the path to success and personal development. Here's an exploration of embracing failure as a learning opportunity:

Cultivating a Growth Mindset: Embracing failure as a learning opportunity begins with cultivating a growth mindset— a belief that abilities and intelligence can be developed through dedication and effort. Encouraging individuals to adopt a growth mindset empowers them to view failure as a natural part of the learning process, rather than a reflection of their innate abilities or worth. By embracing challenges and setbacks as opportunities for growth and learning, individuals develop resilience, perseverance, and a willingness to embrace new experiences.

Extracting Lessons and Insights: Embracing failure as a learning opportunity involves extracting valuable lessons and

79

insights from setbacks and mistakes. Encouraging individuals to reflect on their experiences, identify areas for improvement, and glean insights from their failures helps them extract meaning and wisdom from challenging circumstances. By viewing failure as a source of valuable feedback and information, individuals gain clarity, insight, and perspective on their journey towards personal and professional growth.

Fostering Resilience and Adaptability: Embracing failure as a learning opportunity fosters resilience and adaptability in the face of adversity. Encouraging individuals to bounce back from setbacks, learn from mistakes, and adapt their strategies empowers them to overcome obstacles and thrive amidst challenges. By reframing failure as a temporary setback rather than a permanent defeat, individuals develop the resilience and perseverance needed to navigate through life's ups and downs with courage and determination.

Promoting Innovation and Creativity: Embracing failure as a learning opportunity promotes innovation and creativity by encouraging individuals to take risks and explore new ideas. Encouraging individuals to step outside their comfort zones, experiment with different approaches, and embrace uncertainty fosters a culture of innovation and growth. By viewing failure as a natural byproduct of experimentation and exploration, individuals unleash their creative potential and discover new solutions to old problems.

Cultivating Self-Compassion and Self-Empathy: Embracing failure as a learning opportunity involves cultivating self-compassion and self-empathy towards oneself. Encouraging individuals to treat themselves with kindness, understanding, and acceptance during times of failure helps them navigate through disappointment and setbacks with resilience and grace. By practicing self-compassion, individuals develop the inner strength and self-worth needed to persevere in the face of adversity.

Developing a Growth Mindset towards Setbacks

In "Switch Your Mind: Steps to Take When You Are Faced with Trial and in Times of

Challenges," the cultivation of a growth mindset towards setbacks emerges as a fundamental principle for navigating adversity with resilience, clarity, and growth. A growth mindset empowers individuals to perceive setbacks as opportunities for learning, development, and personal growth, rather than as insurmountable obstacles. Here's an exploration of developing a growth mindset towards setbacks:

Understanding the Nature of a Growth Mindset: Developing a growth mindset towards setbacks begins with understanding its core principles. A growth mindset, as coined by psychologist Carol Dweck, is the belief that abilities and intelligence can be developed through dedication, effort, and learning. Individuals with a growth mindset embrace challenges, persist in the face of obstacles, and see failure as a stepping stone to success.

Embracing Challenges as Opportunities: Developing a growth mindset involves embracing challenges as opportunities for growth and learning.

Encouraging individuals to view setbacks as temporary obstacles rather than permanent limitations empowers them to approach adversity with courage, resilience, and determination. By reframing setbacks as opportunities for personal and professional development, individuals cultivate a sense of optimism and empowerment in the face of adversity.

Learning from Failure and Mistakes: Developing a growth mindset towards setbacks entails learning from failure and mistakes. Encouraging individuals to reflect on their experiences, identify areas for improvement, and extract lessons from setbacks helps them grow and evolve. By viewing failure as a natural part of the learning process, individuals develop resilience, perseverance, and a willingness to embrace new challenges.

Embracing Effort and Persistence: Developing a growth mindset involves embracing effort and persistence as essential components of success. Encouraging individuals to approach challenges with a sense of determination, grit, and perseverance empowers them to overcome obstacles and achieve their goals. By recognizing that progress takes time and effort, individuals cultivate resilience and tenacity in the face of adversity.

Seeking Feedback and Support: Developing a growth mindset towards setbacks involves seeking feedback and support from others. Encouraging individuals to seek guidance, mentorship, and constructive criticism helps them gain insights into their strengths and areas for improvement. By embracing feedback as a catalyst for growth and learning, individuals enhance their resilience and adaptability in the face of challenges.

Cultivating Self-Compassion and Self-Empathy: Developing a growth mindset entails cultivating self-compassion and self-empathy towards oneself. Encouraging individuals to treat themselves with kindness, understanding, and acceptance during times of setback helps them navigate through disappointment and failure with resilience and grace. By practicing self-compassion, individuals develop the inner strength and self-worth needed to persevere in the face of adversity.

Finding Meaning and Purpose in Times of Adversity

In "Switch Your Mind: Steps to Take When You Are Faced with Trial and in Times of Challenges," the exploration of finding meaning and purpose in times of adversity emerges as a transformative journey of self-discovery, resilience, and growth. Amidst life's challenges, individuals are empowered to uncover deeper meaning, tap into their inner purpose, and cultivate a sense of fulfillment and direction. Here's an exploration of finding meaning and purpose in times of adversity:

Reflecting on Core Values and Beliefs: Finding meaning and purpose in times of adversity begins with reflecting on core values and beliefs. Encouraging individuals to connect with what truly matters to them whether it's relationships, personal growth, making a positive impact, or spiritual fulfillment helps them anchor themselves amidst life's storms. By aligning their actions with their values and beliefs, individuals find clarity and direction in the face of adversity.

Identifying Growth Opportunities and Lessons: Finding meaning and purpose involves identifying growth opportunities and lessons within adversity. Encouraging individuals to search for silver linings, lessons learned, and opportunities for personal and professional development helps them derive meaning from challenging circumstances. By reframing setbacks as opportunities for growth and learning, individuals transform adversity into a catalyst for personal transformation and empowerment.

Connecting with Personal Strengths and Passions: Finding meaning and purpose entails connecting with personal strengths, passions, and interests. Encouraging individuals to explore their talents, interests, and passions helps them uncover their unique gifts and contributions to the world. By engaging in activities that ignite their enthusiasm and bring them joy, individuals cultivate a sense of purpose and fulfillment amidst life's challenges.

Making a Positive Impact and Contribution: Finding meaning and purpose involves making a positive impact and contribution to others and the world. Encouraging individuals to seek opportunities to serve, help, and uplift others fosters a sense of connection, empathy, and fulfillment. By making a difference in the lives of others, individuals find meaning and purpose beyond their personal struggles, contributing to a greater sense of well-being and fulfillment.

Embracing the Journey of Self-Discovery and Growth: Finding meaning and purpose is ultimately a journey of self-discovery and growth. Encouraging individuals to embrace the journey with openness, curiosity, and courage allows them to explore new possibilities, overcome limiting beliefs, and tap into their full potential. By viewing adversity as a pathway to self-discovery and growth, individuals emerge stronger, wiser, and more empowered than before.

Cultivating Gratitude and Resilience: Finding meaning and purpose involves cultivating gratitude and resilience in the face of adversity. Encouraging individuals to practice gratitude for the blessings and lessons in their lives helps them shift their focus from scarcity to abundance. By cultivating resilience, individuals develop the inner strength and perseverance needed to navigate through challenges with courage and grace.

CHAPTER 6

CASE STUDIES AND REAL-LIFE EXAMPLES

Integrating Case Studies and Real-Life Examples into "Switch Your Mind: Steps to Take When You Are Faced with Trial and in Times of Challenges" enriches the content and enhances its practical relevance for readers. By weaving in relatable narratives and tangible experiences, the book becomes more engaging, insightful, and actionable. Here's how case studies and real-life examples can be incorporated:

Illustrating Resilience in Action: Introduce case studies featuring individuals who have demonstrated resilience in the face of adversity. Share stories of overcoming significant challenges, such as illness, loss, career setbacks, or personal crises. Highlight the strategies and mindset shifts these individuals employed to navigate through adversity, showcasing the transformative power of resilience.

Highlighting Diverse Perspectives:
Include real-life examples that reflect diverse experiences and perspectives. Showcase stories from different cultural backgrounds, ages, professions, and life circumstances to illustrate the universality of human resilience. By highlighting diverse narratives, readers gain insights into the various ways individuals navigate through challenges and cultivate resilience.

Demonstrating Practical Strategies:
Integrate case studies that exemplify the practical strategies outlined in the book. Share stories of individuals who have applied mindfulness techniques, mindset shifts, coping mechanisms, and self-care practices to navigate through difficult times. Provide concrete examples of how these strategies were implemented and the impact they had on individuals' well-being and resilience.

Inspiring Personal Transformation:
Share stories of personal transformation and growth resulting from adversity. Feature individuals who have turned setbacks into opportunities for self-discovery, purposeful living, and meaningful contribution. Illustrate how

challenges can serve as catalysts for positive change and inner fulfillment, inspiring readers to embrace their own journey of growth and resilience.

Offering Empathy and Validation: Incorporate real-life examples that offer empathy and validation to readers facing similar challenges. Share stories of struggle, doubt, and uncertainty to reassure readers that they are not alone in their experiences. Highlight the resilience and strength exhibited by individuals navigating through similar circumstances, providing hope and encouragement to those in need.

Facilitating Learning and Application: Conclude each chapter with reflective questions or prompts based on the case studies and real-life examples shared. Encourage readers to relate these stories to their own lives, consider how they would respond in similar situations, and identify actionable steps they can take to enhance their resilience and well-being.

Personal Stories of Overcoming Challenges

Trekking to and Fro University to my home: A Story of Resilience

During my university days, one of the most challenging yet transformative experiences was the daily trek to and from school. Living far from campus meant enduring long walks, unpredictable weather, and logistical hurdles. However, this journey became a testament to resilience, determination, and the power of mindset.

Each morning, rain or shine, I embarked on the trek, armed with determination and a positive outlook. The initial steps were daunting, especially on gloomy days when motivation waned. Yet, with each stride, I reminded myself of the purpose behind the journey to pursue education, expand horizons, and chase dreams.

The trek offered moments of solitude amidst bustling city life. As I walked, thoughts swirled, reflecting on challenges faced and goals pursued. Each step symbolized progress, resilience, and a refusal to succumb to adversity. The physical exertion mirrored the mental fortitude required to navigate through life's obstacles.

The journey wasn't without its trials. There were days when fatigue threatened to overwhelm, and doubts crept in. Yet, in those moments, I drew strength from the resilience ingrained within a reminder of past triumphs and the potential for future successes.

The return journey mirrored the day's challenges a test of endurance and perseverance. As fatigue set in, each step became a testament to resilience and determination. Yet, amidst physical strain, moments of clarity emerged a reminder of the transformative power of adversity.

Looking back, the daily trek symbolizes more than a physical journey; it embodies resilience, determination, and the unwavering pursuit of goals. Through rain and shine, challenges and triumphs, the journey forged resilience, shaped character, and instilled an unwavering belief in the power of the human spirit.

Case Studies from Various Fields and Industries

In "Switch Your Mind," we explore the transformative power of mindset and resilience in navigating through life's challenges. One effective way to illustrate these concepts is through case studies drawn from various fields and industries. These real-life examples provide insights, inspiration, and practical strategies for overcoming adversity and achieving personal and professional growth. Let's delve into some compelling case studies:

1. Entrepreneurship: Overcoming Failure and Building Resilience

Case Study: Sarah's Journey in Entrepreneurship

Sarah embarked on her entrepreneurial journey with passion and determination, launching a tech startup aimed at revolutionizing the healthcare industry. However, the road to success was fraught with challenges funding constraints, market saturation, and technical setbacks.

Despite initial setbacks and failures, Sarah remained resilient, leveraging each obstacle as a learning opportunity. Through strategic pivots, relentless perseverance, and unwavering belief in her vision, Sarah transformed adversity into opportunity. Today, her startup stands as a testament to resilience, innovation, and the power of a growth mindset in the face of adversity.

2 Healthcare: Navigating Crisis and Cultivating Compassion

Case Study: Dr. Patel's Response to a Global Pandemic

Dr. Patel, a frontline healthcare worker, faced unprecedented challenges during the global pandemic. As hospitals overflowed with patients and resources dwindled, Dr. Patel confronted overwhelming stress, exhaustion, and uncertainty. Yet, amidst the chaos, Dr. Patel remained steadfast in his commitment to patient care, demonstrating resilience, compassion, and leadership in the face of adversity. Through teamwork, adaptability, and unwavering dedication, Dr. Patel and his colleagues navigated through the crisis, saving lives and inspiring hope in the darkest of times.

3. Education: Empowering Students through Adversity Case Study: Maria's Journey to Academic Success

Maria, a first-generation college student, faced numerous obstacles on her path to academic success financial constraints, language barriers, and self-doubt. Yet, fueled by a relentless pursuit of knowledge and a burning desire to create a better future, Maria persevered. Through hard work, resilience, and a growth mindset, Maria excelled academically, surpassing expectations and inspiring others along the way. Today, Maria's journey stands as a testament to the transformative power of education, resilience, and unwavering determination in overcoming adversity.

These case studies illustrate the transformative power of mindset, resilience, and determination in overcoming adversity across various fields and industries. Whether in entrepreneurship, healthcare, education, or beyond, individuals have the capacity to navigate through life's challenges with courage, clarity, and unwavering determination. Through these real-life examples, readers are empowered to embrace the journey towards personal and professional growth, transforming obstacles into opportunities and adversity into triumph.

Introduction to Successful Strategies

In "Switch Your Mind," we explore an array of successful strategies for handling adversity, drawing inspiration from real-life examples, psychological principles, and practical wisdom. By analyzing these strategies, readers gain valuable insights into navigating through life's challenges with resilience, clarity, and empowerment. Let's delve into some effective approaches:

1. Resilience Building

Successful Strategy: Cultivating a Resilient Mindset

Resilience is the ability to bounce back from setbacks, adapt to change, and thrive amidst adversity. Strategies for building resilience include fostering optimism, embracing challenges as opportunities for growth, nurturing social support networks, and practicing self-care and mindfulness techniques. By cultivating a resilient mindset, individuals develop the inner strength and flexibility needed to navigate through life's challenges with courage and grace.

2. Mindset Shifts

Successful Strategy: Adopting a Growth Mindset

A growth mindset is the belief that abilities and intelligence can be developed through dedication and effort. Individuals with a growth mindset view challenges as opportunities for learning, embrace failure as a natural part of the learning process, and persist in the face of obstacles. By adopting a growth mindset, individuals unlock their potential, cultivate resilience, and approach adversity with optimism and determination.

3. Coping Mechanisms

Successful Strategy: Implementing Effective Coping Mechanisms

Coping mechanisms are strategies individuals use to manage stress, regulate emotions, and cope with adversity. Effective coping mechanisms include problem-solving, seeking social support, engaging in relaxation techniques, and reframing negative thoughts. By implementing healthy coping mechanisms, individuals enhance their resilience, maintain emotional well-being, and navigate through challenges with greater ease and clarity.

4. Self-Reflection and Adaptation
Successful Strategy: Engaging in Self-Reflection and Adaptation

Self-reflection involves introspection, mindfulness, and a willingness to examine one's thoughts, emotions, and behaviors. By reflecting on past experiences, identifying patterns, and learning from mistakes, individuals gain insight into their strengths, weaknesses, and areas for growth. Adaptation involves flexibility, openness to change, and a willingness to adjust strategies based on feedback and new information. By engaging in self-reflection and adaptation, individuals enhance their self-awareness, cultivate resilience, and navigate through adversity with greater clarity and purpose.

Successful strategies for handling adversity encompass a range of approaches, from resilience building and mindset shifts to coping mechanisms and self-reflection. By analyzing these strategies and applying them in their own lives, readers of "Switch Your Mind" are empowered to navigate through life's challenges with courage, clarity, and resilience. Through intentional practice and a commitment to personal growth, individuals harness the power of their minds to overcome adversity and thrive in the face of uncertainty.

CHAPTER 7

CREATING A PERSONALIZED ACTION PLAN

Introduction to Creating a Personalized Action Plan

In "Switch Your Mind," the journey towards resilience and empowerment begins with the creation of a personalized action plan tailored to individual needs, goals, and circumstances. By developing a roadmap for navigating through challenges, readers gain clarity, focus, and direction in their journey towards personal growth and transformation. Let's explore the key components of creating a personalized action plan:

Self-Assessment and Reflection

Begin by conducting a thorough self-assessment and reflection on your current circumstances, strengths, weaknesses, and areas for growth. Reflect on past

101

experiences, challenges faced, and lessons learned. Identify patterns, triggers, and barriers to resilience. By gaining insight into your inner landscape, you lay the foundation for meaningful growth and transformation.

Clarifying Goals and Priorities

Next, clarify your goals, values, and priorities. What do you hope to achieve in the face of adversity? What values guide your actions and decisions? Define specific, measurable, and achievable goals that align with your vision for resilience and empowerment. Prioritize your goals based on their significance and relevance to your overall well-being and fulfillment.

Identifying Strategies and Resources

Identify strategies and resources to support your journey towards resilience and empowerment. Draw inspiration from proven techniques such as mindfulness, positive psychology, cognitive-behavioral therapy, and social support networks. Explore resources such as books, articles, workshops, and online communities that resonate with your needs and preferences. By assembling a toolkit of strategies and resources, you empower yourself to navigate through challenges with courage and clarity.

Establishing Actionable Steps

Break down your goals into actionable steps and milestones. What specific actions can you take to move closer to your desired outcomes? Create a detailed action plan with clear timelines, deadlines, and accountability mechanisms. Prioritize tasks based on their importance and feasibility. Celebrate small victories along the way and adjust your plan as needed based on feedback and new information.

Cultivating Accountability and Support

Cultivate accountability and support to maintain momentum and motivation. Share your action plan with trusted friends, family members, or mentors who can provide encouragement, feedback, and accountability. Join support groups or accountability partnerships to stay motivated and connected. By surrounding yourself with a supportive network, you enhance your resilience and commitment to personal growth.

Reflecting and Adjusting

Regularly reflect on your progress, challenges, and insights gained along the way. What strategies are proving effective? What obstacles are hindering your progress? Adjust your action plan as needed based on feedback and self-reflection. Remain flexible and open to new possibilities. Embrace the journey of growth and transformation with curiosity, resilience, and a willingness to learn.

In "Switch Your Mind," creating a personalized action plan serves as a roadmap for navigating through life's challenges with courage, clarity, and empowerment. By conducting self-assessment and reflection, clarifying goals and priorities, identifying strategies and resources, establishing actionable steps, cultivating accountability and support, and reflecting and adjusting along the way, readers embark on a transformative journey towards resilience and empowerment. Through intentional action and a commitment to personal growth, individuals harness the power of their minds to overcome adversity and thrive in the face of uncertainty.

CHAPTER 8
SETTING SMART GOALS FOR OVERCOMING CHALLENGES

In "Switch Your Mind," setting SMART goals serves as a foundational step in the journey towards overcoming challenges with resilience and clarity. By establishing goals that are Specific, Measurable, Achievable, Relevant, and Time-bound, readers gain focus, motivation, and direction in their pursuit of personal growth and empowerment. Let's explore the process of setting SMART goals for overcoming challenges:

Specificity: Define Clear and Specific Goals

Begin by defining clear and specific goals that articulate what you aim to achieve in the face of adversity. Be specific about the desired outcome, identifying who, what, when, where, and why of your goal. For example, instead of setting a vague goal like "Improve my mental health," specify "Practice mindfulness meditation for 15 minutes daily to reduce stress and anxiety."

Measurability: Establish Concrete Metrics for Success

Ensure that your goals are measurable, allowing you to track progress and evaluate success objectively. Define concrete metrics or indicators that enable you to measure your progress towards the goal. Quantify the desired outcome whenever possible, whether it's tracking the number of meditation sessions completed or monitoring changes in stress levels over time.

Achievability: Set Goals that are Realistic and Attainable

Set goals that are realistic and attainable, considering your current circumstances, resources, and capabilities. Assess the feasibility of achieving the goal within the given timeframe and with available resources. Set challenging yet realistic goals that stretch your abilities without overwhelming you. Break larger goals into smaller, manageable tasks to enhance achievability.

Relevance: Ensure Goals Align with Your Values and Priorities

Ensure that your goals align with your values, priorities, and overarching objectives. Assess the relevance of each goal to your long-term vision for personal growth and well-being. Consider how achieving the goal contributes to your overall sense of fulfillment and empowerment. Align goals with your values to ensure they resonate deeply and inspire meaningful action.

Time-Bound: Establish Clear Deadlines and Timeframes

Establish clear deadlines and timeframes for achieving your goals, providing a sense of urgency and accountability. Define specific target dates or milestones by which you aim to accomplish the goal. Break down larger goals into smaller, time-bound objectives to maintain momentum and focus. Regularly review and adjust deadlines as needed to ensure progress remains on track.

In "Switch Your Mind," setting SMART goals serves as a powerful strategy for overcoming challenges with resilience and clarity. By establishing goals that are Specific, Measurable, Achievable, Relevant, and Time-bound, readers gain focus, motivation, and direction in their journey towards personal growth and empowerment. Through intentional goal-setting and a commitment to action, individuals harness the power of their minds to overcome adversity and thrive in the face of uncertainty.

Identifying Key Areas for Improvement

Identifying Key Areas for Improvement

In "Switch Your Mind," the process of identifying key areas for improvement serves as a foundational step in the journey towards personal growth, resilience, and empowerment. By identifying areas where growth and development are needed, readers gain clarity, insight, and direction in their pursuit of overcoming challenges and thriving amidst adversity. Let's explore the process of identifying key areas for improvement:

Self-Reflection and Assessment

Begin by engaging in self-reflection and assessment of your current circumstances, strengths, weaknesses, and areas for growth. Reflect on past experiences, challenges faced, and lessons learned. Identify patterns, triggers, and barriers to resilience and well-being. By gaining insight into your inner landscape, you lay the groundwork for meaningful growth and transformation.

Clarifying Goals and Aspirations

Clarify your goals, aspirations, and vision for personal growth and fulfillment. What areas of your life do you aspire to improve? What values and priorities guide your actions and decisions? Define specific, meaningful goals that align with your vision for resilience and empowerment. Prioritize goals based on their significance and relevance to your overall well-being and fulfillment.

Seeking Feedback and Perspective

Seek feedback and perspective from trusted friends, mentors, or colleagues who can offer valuable insights and observations. Ask for constructive feedback on areas where you can improve and grow. Be open to different perspectives and viewpoints, recognizing that feedback serves as a catalyst for growth and self-awareness. Embrace feedback as an opportunity for learning and development.

Assessing Skills and Competencies

Assess your skills, competencies, and areas of expertise across various domains of your life. Identify strengths that you can leverage to overcome challenges and achieve your goals. Acknowledge areas where skill development or enhancement is needed to thrive in your personal and professional endeavors. By assessing your skills objectively, you gain clarity on areas for improvement and growth.

Identifying Patterns and Habits

Identify patterns and habits that may be contributing to challenges or hindering your progress. Reflect on recurring behaviors, thought patterns, and routines that impact your well-being and effectiveness. Are there habits that you need to change or cultivate to support your goals and aspirations? By identifying patterns and habits, you empower yourself to make intentional choices and adjustments.

Prioritizing Areas for Growth

Prioritize key areas for growth and improvement based on their impact on your overall well-being and fulfillment. Focus on areas where change and development will yield the greatest benefits and outcomes. Break down larger goals into smaller, actionable steps that you can take to facilitate progress and momentum. By prioritizing areas for growth, you create a roadmap for meaningful transformation and empowerment.

In "Switch Your Mind," the process of identifying key areas for improvement serves as a transformative journey towards personal growth, resilience, and empowerment. By engaging in self-reflection, clarifying goals, seeking feedback, assessing skills, identifying patterns, and prioritizing areas for growth, readers embark on a path of self-discovery and transformation. Through intentional effort and a commitment to improvement, individuals harness the power of their minds to overcome challenges and thrive in the face of adversity.

CHAPTER 9

DEVELOPING A STEP-BY-STEP ACTION PLAN FOR MINDSET TRANSFORMATION

Mindset Transformation

In "Switch Your Mind," mindset transformation serves as a powerful catalyst for navigating through life's challenges with resilience, clarity, and empowerment. By developing a step-by-step action plan for mindset transformation, readers embark on a transformative journey towards personal growth and empowerment. Let's explore the process of developing an action plan for mindset transformation:

Self-Reflection and Awareness

Begin by engaging in self-reflection and cultivating awareness of your current mindset and belief systems. Reflect on your thoughts, attitudes, and perceptions towards challenges and adversity. Identify limiting beliefs, negative thought patterns, and cognitive distortions that may be hindering your growth and well-being. By gaining insight into your mindset, you lay the foundation for meaningful transformation.

Clarifying Desired Mindset

Clarify the desired mindset you wish to cultivate in the face of adversity. Define the qualities, attitudes, and beliefs that align with resilience, positivity, and empowerment. Visualize the ideal mindset you aspire to embody and the impact it will have on your ability to navigate challenges with courage and clarity. Set clear intentions for mindset transformation based on your vision for personal growth and well-being.

Setting Specific Goals for Mindset Transformation

Set specific goals for mindset transformation that are aligned with your desired outcomes and priorities. Define actionable steps and milestones for cultivating a resilient and empowered mindset. Break down larger goals into smaller, manageable tasks that you can integrate into your daily routine. Ensure that goals are SMART (Specific, Measurable, Achievable, Relevant, and Time-bound) to maintain focus and accountability.

Identifying Trigger Points and Challenges

Identify trigger points and challenges that may undermine your efforts towards mindset transformation. Recognize situations, environments, or individuals that evoke negative emotions, self-doubt, or resistance to change. Anticipate potential obstacles and develop strategies for managing triggers effectively. Cultivate resilience and self-awareness to navigate through challenges with grace and perseverance.

Implementing Mindfulness and Cognitive Strategies

Implement mindfulness and cognitive strategies to facilitate mindset transformation. Practice mindfulness meditation, deep breathing exercises, or visualization techniques to cultivate present-moment awareness and emotional regulation. Challenge negative thought patterns and cognitive distortions through cognitive restructuring and reframing techniques. Cultivate a growth mindset by embracing challenges as opportunities for learning and growth.

Cultivating Support and Accountability

Cultivate support and accountability to sustain momentum and motivation in your journey towards mindset transformation. Share your goals and intentions with trusted friends, family members, or mentors who can provide encouragement, feedback, and accountability. Join support groups or coaching programs that offer guidance, inspiration, and community. Celebrate progress and milestones along the way, recognizing the power of support in fostering growth and resilience.

In "Switch Your Mind," developing a step-by-step action plan for mindset transformation empowers readers to navigate through life's challenges with courage, clarity, and empowerment. By engaging in self-reflection, clarifying desired mindset, setting specific goals, identifying trigger points, implementing mindfulness and cognitive strategies, and cultivating support and accountability, individuals embark on a transformative journey towards personal growth and resilience. Through intentional effort and a commitment to mindset transformation, readers harness the power of their minds to overcome adversity and thrive in the face of uncertainty.

Tracking Progress and Celebrating Milestones

Tracking Progress and Celebrating Milestones

In "Switch Your Mind," tracking progress and celebrating milestones play a vital role in maintaining motivation, fostering resilience, and sustaining momentum on the journey towards personal growth and empowerment. By acknowledging and celebrating each step forward, readers cultivate a sense of accomplishment, optimism, and self-efficacy. Let's explore the significance of tracking progress and celebrating milestones:

Setting Clear Metrics for Progress

Begin by setting clear metrics and indicators for tracking progress towards your goals. Define specific criteria and milestones that signify meaningful progress and achievement. Whether it's the number of mindfulness sessions completed, the reduction in stress levels, or the completion of action steps towards mindset transformation, establish tangible markers that reflect your journey towards resilience and empowerment.

Establishing Tracking Systems and Tools

Establish tracking systems and tools to monitor your progress effectively. Utilize journals, apps, spreadsheets, or online platforms to record and track your daily or weekly activities, accomplishments, and insights. Regularly review your progress against established metrics and adjust your strategies as needed. By maintaining visibility into your journey, you gain clarity and accountability in pursuing your goals.

Reflecting on Insights and Learnings

Take time to reflect on insights, learnings, and lessons gained throughout your journey. Pause to acknowledge the challenges you've overcome, the growth you've experienced, and the insights you've gained along the way. Reflect on the strategies that have been effective in supporting your progress and identify areas for refinement or adjustment. By embracing a mindset of continuous learning and reflection, you deepen your understanding of yourself and your capabilities.

Celebrating Achievements and Milestones

Celebrate achievements and milestones as you progress towards your goals. Take time to acknowledge and celebrate each step forward, no matter how small or incremental it may seem. Celebrate moments of resilience, courage, and perseverance in the face of adversity. Whether it's treating yourself to a small reward, sharing your accomplishments with loved ones, or simply pausing to savor the moment, find meaningful ways to honor your progress and achievements.

Cultivating Gratitude and Positivity

Cultivate gratitude and positivity as you reflect on your journey and celebrate milestones. Express gratitude for the progress you've made, the support you've received, and the opportunities for growth and learning. Embrace a positive outlook as you face challenges and setbacks, recognizing them as opportunities for growth and resilience. By fostering a mindset of gratitude and positivity, you cultivate resilience and optimism in the face of adversity.

Revisiting Goals and Setting New Milestones

Periodically revisit your goals, reassess your progress, and set new milestones to keep your journey dynamic and engaging. Reflect on your evolving aspirations, priorities, and values, and adjust your goals accordingly. Celebrate the achievement of major milestones and use them as springboards for setting new, ambitious objectives. Embrace the journey of growth and transformation with curiosity, enthusiasm, and a commitment to continuous improvement.

In "Switch Your Mind," tracking progress and celebrating milestones serve as essential components of the journey towards personal growth and empowerment. By setting clear metrics, establishing tracking systems, reflecting on insights, celebrating achievements, cultivating gratitude, and revisiting goals, readers maintain momentum and motivation in navigating through life's challenges with resilience and clarity. Through intentional effort and a commitment to progress, individuals harness the power of their minds to overcome adversity and thrive in the face of uncertainty.

CHAPTER 10

CONCLUSION: EMPOWERING YOUR JOURNEY

In concluding our exploration of "Switch Your Mind: Steps to Take When You Are Faced with Trial and in Time of Challenges," it's essential to reflect on the transformative insights and empowering strategies we've uncovered together. Throughout this journey, we've delved into the depths of the human psyche, discovering the power of mindset in shaping our responses to adversity.

Summarizing Key Takeaways from the Book

We've learned that resilience isn't just a trait; it's a skill that can be cultivated and strengthened through intentional practice. By adopting a growth mindset, we can reframe challenges as opportunities for growth and learning. Through mindfulness techniques, cognitive strategies, and positive affirmations, we can harness the power of our minds to navigate through life's trials with courage and clarity.

Encouragement for Continued Growth and Development

As you continue your journey beyond these pages, I encourage you to embrace the principles and practices shared in this book. Remember that transformation is a journey, not a destination. It requires patience, perseverance, and a commitment to self-discovery. Celebrate your progress, no matter how small, and embrace setbacks as opportunities for growth. Trust in your resilience, and believe in your capacity to overcome any obstacle that stands in your path.

Final Thoughts and Words of Inspiration

In the face of adversity, remember that you are not alone. Draw strength from the knowledge that countless others have walked this path before you, overcoming challenges with grace and resilience. Trust in your inner wisdom, and listen to the whispers of your heart. Believe in the power of your dreams, and never lose sight of the infinite possibilities that lie ahead.

As you navigate the twists and turns of life's journey, may you always remember the resilience that resides within you? May you embrace each new challenge as an opportunity for growth and transformation? And may you always hold fast to the belief that no matter how dark the night may seem, the dawn of a new day is always on the horizon.

Thank you for entrusting me with a small part of your journey. As you continue to walk your path, may you do so with courage, conviction, and unwavering faith in the power of your mind to overcome any obstacle that comes your way?

OTHER BOOKS BY THE AUTHOR

https://www.amazon.com/author/henryeparkins